THE ART OF CRAFTING A BOOK

TECHNIQUES FOR GREAT WRITING

FARAH KURESHI

Table of Contents

Introduction 1

Chapter 1: The Art of Crafting A Book 3

Chapter 2: The Beginnings of Your Book 13

Chapter 3: The Creative Process 22

Chapter 4: Themes and Sentence Structure 33

Chapter 5: How To Develop Your Writing Abilities 42

Chapter 6: Fears And Anxieties Regarding Writing 49

Chapter 7: Believing in your writing abilities 56

Chapter 8: Enhancing Your Writing Abilities 66

Chapter 9: Staying True to Yourself 74

Introduction

Have you always dreamed of being a writer or writing a book? Did the process seem incredibly difficult for you to do? Take no heed you're not the only one! Many people find writing to be a difficult challenge, and it is. Most writers spend their time crafting their art.

Writing is not as difficult as it seems, though the process can be time-consuming and a lot of hard work. It takes dedication, hard work and practice to craft your skill of becoming a successful and talented writer. Writing a book may seem like a difficult task and feat, but it's not as hard as it seems and becomes easier with time. You may not be a natural writer or possess natural talent, but you still have the ability to learn effective writing techniques and various processes for being a better writer and honing your technique and ability. You may also have natural talent so being a writer is generally easier for you, but you still may need to develop your skills and craft and become a great and talented success you were meant to be.

The choice of writing can come with many different obstacles and hazards. There are many challenges writers out there face such as writers block, the fear of criticism, and the fear of being mediocre or not doing as well as they thought they would do as a writing talent. There are so many different aspects out there that entail or encompass the concept of writing and there is also a lot of competition out there when it comes to the process of writing. There are thousands of fellow writers out there attempting to become great talents and greats and spread their knowledge and work around the world. It's easy to get caught up in the writing trap and lose your sense of self, so it's very important to stay true to yourself during your writing journey.

You'll want to learn how to create great results for yourself by staying confident, not letting others bring you down, and escalating yourself in the creative process in order to get ahead as a writer. Hopefully you will be able to do these things after reading this book and learning the different techniques present in it.

Chapter 1

The Art of Crafting A Book

Have you ever written a manuscript? Dreamed of writing a book in your life? Did you feel writing a book was more difficult than you can imagine and was too scared of the situation to put one together? Take no heed! Writing a book is a gifted and given artform that many people have achieved, yet there are a number of people out there who find the concept too overwhelming and daunting to tackle. It may not be as difficult as you think though, for there are methods and practices that will allow you to far easily put one together and once you do so a few times, will be able to do with greater ease.

Writing a book is not an easy task- it is something that can take years of practice or even natural abilities of writing to be able to do in the first place. Writing a book is a difficult activity and is work for a person, though it's something that becomes easier as time goes by and as a person becomes gifted with the ability to write better by writing more. It can be a wonderful achievement and great success which most people out there are unable to do, and it's something that is an amazing feature to showcase in one's personal life and world and a huge accomplishment.

Crafting a book is a beautiful art that most people can't usually do or fully understand but it is akin to artwork that a person commits to and something that is beautiful, wondrous and that brings forth happiness to those around them. A book is a work of art that is carefully crafted by the author and embossed in varieties of themes, ideas and concoctions that can present as something that is all too amazing to be able to behold.

Books are important treasures that people create and put together in order to inspire, teach, and help people to grow in different forms. They are a wealth of knowledge, wisdom, entertainment, and are a studious way to pass the time and increase your mental strength and capacity. Not every person has the capability or ability to put together a book, but most people do have the ability to learn how to do this difficult and wonderful feat.

Have you always wanted to write a book but found it to be too overwhelming or difficult? Have you dreamed of publishing your work, but it seemed like something you were unable to do? Don't worry- you're not the only one! Many people feel as if publishing a book is just too difficult to even be able to take on as a task, and most people who do try to publish books, end up failing but by not finishing or being able to finish due to the difficulty involved. However, writing a book isn't as difficult as it seems. It takes some brainstorming, being able to write effectively and come up with great ideas, themes and stories and being able to put it all together and takes patience to be able to sit in front of a computer and put words and stories together in order to influence, entertain, and inspire others.

Most writers often feel as if once they publish a book they're destined for fame and fortune as writers or that they will be widely known. They feel as if people will automatically know who they are yet little do they know that this is far from the truth. Publishing a book is a difficult task and is a wonderful achievement for any given individual, but an unknown person isn't going to be just known for publishing their work on amazon or some place online. It may take years of hard working and effective marketing strategies for a person to be known for their brilliant hard work and for someone to be well-known as an author or even recognized or established.

Being a writer can be a difficult but gifted feat. I once was a writer but didn't hone into my writing abilities. I knew I always wanted to write books and articles but never thought or cared to do this. Things have changed drastically now, for I am now writing books and publishing them to the best of my ability and have plans to write more and do more in order to help people and teach them the things I do know. Writing takes talent and ability, and it isn't as difficult as people consider or think it to be. If you want to be a writer, you truly can do so, but you must believe in yourself and understand the craft and how it works and how you too can put together a book and come up with words, ideas, phrases and amazing thoughts and be able to allow them to flow through you seamlessly without a problem or issue.

Writing is a beautiful, amazing gift that many people do possess. Not everyone has these abilities and though they can be learned, it also should come naturally for many people who want to participate or partake in the craft. Now of course this doesn't mean that a person can't learn the art of writing. Anyone can really, and they too can develop these abilities that may come innately for some and grow and become better writers and people who are easily inspired to be able to write, learn and grow from this process.

Writing more and more can assist a person into being a better writer. It can really help you into becoming a better and gifted writer and person. With writing comes the art of practice and the means of allowing a writer the talented ability to be able to grow as a writer with each work they put together, create, connect with and publish. As a writer writes more, they will become better at their craft and will one day be able to teach and help others to become better as well.

What have you written so far in your life? Have you written essays, articles? Have you done workshops in writing? Are you an expert writer already who simply has not written a book yet? Writing a book can be a huge challenge for most people, even for those who are experts in writing. There are many people out there who have been writing for many years. They have never written a book or put one together. Many people feel as if putting a book together is the most difficult challenge for a person to do. This may be the case for many people, however, the truth is that no matter what level of writer you are, once you finally write one book or put one book together you have finally accomplished this amazing great goal, and it's something that becomes that can become much easier for you once you do it the first time.

You will need to understand that writing a book is really not as difficult as it seems to be, for once you do it once or twice then you will grow in to becoming a master at it or much better than you were and it will become much easier for you to write more and more books and the more books you write the easier the process will become and pretty soon it will seem like a very simple process for you to do.

The beginnings of being a writer

Does it take amazing grammatical skill to become a writer? How do people write so effectively and efficiently and how on earth do people write long novels of hundreds and thousands of words? Well, this can be answered in many different ways. People who are naturally gifted at the art are able to write long books and articles as they please. They are able to commit to the art of writing only because they are innately naturally gifted writers and are able to put together pieces of work very efficiently and much easily than a person could comprehend. There are, however, others who might find doing so a little bit more of a challenge and may find it takes them more time to put together a piece or they may be writing as a part-time short hobby on the side and aren't spending most of their efforts in the art of attempting to put together a piece of work or an article.

It is good to practice writing, work hard and diligently and become true to your craft. The more you practice and write, the better you will become at it and the harder you work at practicing this skill the easier it becomes.

What should I write?

Many people might be confused as to how they should start writing and what kind of books or pieces they would need to start off writing with. They may want to start off writing a short novella, a book, a small article, or one good way a person can start off writing with is by going to a website called hub pages or Wattpad and begin writing essays. Sometimes it takes practice to be able to write these essays and writing these essays will give you very good practice when it comes to being able to write in general. Writing takes skill, time, practice and many other concepts that not many people feel they have in general. It takes a lot of patience too and time for a person to be able to put together ideas, concepts, words, thoughts and phrases in order to be able to fully put together a book, article or other paraphernalia they are writing about.

Being a writer is a beautiful, wonderful gift that a person can fully appreciate once they've gained the knack for it and once, they know exactly what they are doing as far as being the kind of writer they seek to be and working hard towards achieving their goals and success in this area.

I enjoy writing and find it a daunting feat and something that gives me joy and happiness and an area where I can use my knowledge and abilities to actually help others and allow my writing to be utilized for the greater good of humanity which is my ultimate purpose in life.

What is your purpose for writing? Do you want to write to entertain people, or do you aim to write to help people in their everyday lives? You'll need to figure out what your purpose for writing is and what your aim in everyday life is. Do you seek to entertain people through fictional novels, non-fictional work, or would you rather write to help people or do you have other reasons for wanting to write. You'll want to figure out the genre of writing you're interested in doing.

Fictional genres are wonderful means of being able to write and entertain the masses. People enjoy and love writing fictional novels and are thrilled to be able to put together interesting, reflective stories full of illuminated characters and situations. Being a fictional writer is a blessed gift and something that is very fun for the people being entertained and for the author as well. Non-fictional type self-help books are great books to write as well for they can help others as well as entertain them and gives people the tools to be able to help themselves in many different circumstances.

Writing a book can be a full-time task for someone or it can be a part-time hobby. For many people writing is subject to their current lifestyle and they have decided how to be an effective writer and how to use their talents and gifts. If you decide to go full-time for writing, then you'll want to know that you can fully utilize your writing talents and abilities as best you can to write the maximum amount of information and do the most work. You'll want to take effective breaks though as people who write tend to become engulfed in their writing and don't give themselves ample enough time to rest and relax from doing their work.

If writing is a part-time hobby for you, then good for you, for writing as a part-time hobby is a wonderful task and is something you'll want to partake in while holding a job and living your life the way you desire it to be. As a part-time writer, you probably won't be able to complete your book as fast as a full-time writer will, but you'll still be able to work on it and grow into becoming a better and better writer. Writing is an excellent hobby to take up and a great lifestyle and something that you'll always cherish, and it can also help you grow in other areas of your life. It can develop your confidence and social skills and allow you to gain the confidence you may have lost in your life. It helps you pursue this goal and allows you to gain the confidence to pursue others goals you may harness in your world.

Being a writer is a very enjoyable thing and task and many writers enjoy great success in their lives by utilizing their gifts to the best of their abilities. There are writers who use their books and abilities to go into public speaking, article writing, give talks, help others, and do much more as authors, for as an author the sky is the limit for you. Writing is a gift and a very wonderful hobby, art, and career to be a part of and undertaking it allows a person to be able to accomplish harmonious growth, pleasure, and happiness as a result of being a talented writer.

CHAPTER 2

The Beginnings of Your Book

Your book should be your own personal and important spiritual, moral, religious, beautiful, and harmonious journey and artwork. A book of course, is a piece of art that is put together through words, thoughts, feelings and emotions and is there for people to experience and to read. Your book should be a heartfelt relay of your own thoughts, feelings, emotions and everything you want to represent in a collection of works for others to read and to be inspired by. Are you seeking to teach others things? What exactly are you good at and what kind of knowledge do you possess? You'll need to figure out what you want to present to others, and what subjects or matters you will want to teach others by and then decide what subjects and genres you want to showcase to the world.

A book is a beautiful subjective work of art that represents your innermost feelings, thoughts, wants, needs, desires, teachings etc. Your book should be reflective of the kind of person you are and the knowledge you've obtained about life and other aspects in your world, the journey you've been through, and all the lessons you've learned. It should showcase your talents, abilities and the message you desire to relay across to others and to the world of readers who will be a part of it.

If you want to be a fictional writer, then you'll want to think of storylines, characters and plots, and themes that you'll seek to write about and the kinds of books you want to represent to others. Fictional writers are different from non-fictional and self-help book writers for they have to create characters, plots, storylines and the books they write are of a very different nature than other books. You'll want to decide what kind of book you would like to write and then go on from there and and begin the writing process for your works of art.

What relaxes you and inspires you? You'll want to sit down and think of the things in your life that relax you and use those to make sure you start off the process of being a writer by relaxing yourself and thinking of the right ideas you have in mind for your particular book. Write down your thoughts and ideas on a computer or piece of paper and go from there. The secret to being a good writer is that once you begin writing, you get better and better at it and can actually write more and more books, articles or what is that you're planning on writing. The more work you do, the better things get for you and you'll want to continue writing in order to practice your skill and develop your art.

You are a genius and an artistic creative person. you'll want to inspire yourself by incorporating positive affirmations in your everyday world simply to bring up yourself and your life and to do good for yourself and be a positive uplifting person and raise your confidence levels. Your self-esteem is very important in a situation like this because in order to be a writer, you'll need to have full confidence in yourself and your abilities and harbor a decent amount of self-esteem. Sometimes writing isn't easy for beginners who don't have the right experience, and they may not know exactly how or what to write and as a result may even quit or stop the writing process altogether.

You'll want to bring up your self-esteem by calling yourself intelligent, beautiful, special and want to make sure that your self-esteem and confidence is at its highest. You also will want to remind yourself to be resilient because being an author isn't an easy task. There are people who might love your work, and others who may not like it at all. You might get negative reviews and find out that there are negative situations that arise sometimes when it comes to being an author, but you can rise above these situations easily.

Writing a book is a big deal. It's not child's play or something to be taken lightly. It's not easy to write a book and it's a daunting and difficult thing that not everyone has the capability to do, so while in the writing process you'll want to pat yourself on the back every so often for being able to put together a book that most people can't even comprehend doing so.

Once you're a published author, you'll be an author for life. You're finally someone who has written a book and has done an excellent and amazing job of doing this very task. You can finally pat yourself on the back and call yourself a published author and internally reflect over the work you've put into the book you've created. You also can be on your way to accomplishing this same task again by starting work on a second book. It's not unheard of to be working on several books at a time and once you've published one book, you can easily work on other books together if you'd like to do so.

There are several steps you'll want to utilize when it comes to writing your book. These include

Decide what you want to write about

Think of an idea, subject and theme

Think of an idea, a subject and a theme you'd like to write about. Brainstorm these ideas and put them together on paper or computer. Make sure to have several different ideas at hand in order to successfully be able to create the best artwork for yourself.

Think of a good cover idea you'll want to utilize

Think of a cover idea you'll want to use for your book. The manuscript is the most important part for now, but a lot of the time you will want to come up with a good book cover or an idea of what you want it to look like and can submit it to someone to create it for you, or if you have the tools can create it for yourself.

Focus on the characters and creations you'll use in the book

Focus on the characters you'll want to create for the book, and the different personalities they might have and begin to write it all down. You can come up with different ideas and create characters if you're doing a fictional book and make sure to give yourself room to revise in case that is needed.

Build a plot and storyline

You'll want to build a plot and storyline for your book. This depends on the kind of book this is and what exactly you're wanting to write about and put together. Are you writing a fictional work of art or a non-fiction book? You can come together with your ideas and think of the best way you'd like to put your story together.

Think of chapters you'll want to put together

Think of chapters and titles you'll want to use. Once you have a theme that you have thought of and a storyline and idea, you will want to create chapters and titles for your outline. Once this is done, you can easily then begin to fill in the blanks and write more for your book and slowly create and develop the internal portion of it and make it come to life! Your chapters will help and assist you with thinking of what exactly to write about in those chapters as well.

As a writer, you'll generally want to be the best writer you can be and many writers in fact write their works with the concept of wanting them to be masterpieces that are flawless and want works of perfection. This will generally be the case for most people. One minor aspect of being an author is the fact that most people who end up being authors automatically feel as if their work will be instantly recognized by others and that they'll suddenly become known by the general public online or that their works are easily found online. This isn't the case, for in order for a person to have their works found online, they will need to be an established author in some form and will have to have a following sometimes for many years or an established following in order to be known and for people to find their creative works of art online or anywhere.

In order to be a known author and get readers, it takes a lot of time, practice and patience for this to occur. You'll also expect to get many reviews but in many cases, you may not get reviews for your work. Sometimes, it takes thousands of people reading your works in order to generate just a few reviews, but most writers aren't aware of this.

Organizing The Chapters

Organizing the chapters of your book is an incredibly important part of the writing process when it comes to putting a book together. You'll want to think about chapters and understand the concept of knowing how to give yourself ideas when it comes to creating chapters and titles for your masterpiece of work. Chapters are the title headings for books and for some it may seem like a difficult task to do. When I first began writing, it seemed very difficult for me to put chapters of all things together. I was very confused at first and unsure of how to do this. I thought- how on earth can I think of words and chapters and headings to think of for a book. However, once I began writing, this became much easier for me and something that became much more fun to do as well.

For instance, if your book is going to be a self-help book about teaching, you'll want to write down an outline of different things you plan on writing about. When I write, I rarely have an outline except for my chapters and write as I go along, but many people tend to use outlines for their books. It's a good idea to write out a good and decent outline for the book you're writing about and the different ideas and themes. Once you have a good outline written or the beginning of an outline, you can begin creating chapters for your book. You'll want to create the chapter title for the outline that you've created. Most of the time, the idea will just come to you of course, but you can attempt to utilize different methods for thinking of chapter titles.

The chapters of your book should be interesting and stay true to the subject at hand. What you write is important and special and it is your special artwork. Your gifts and talents are of major importance to others and to yourself and by writing a book you are spreading your gifts to others and allowing them to learn the knowledge you utilize and possess within yourself. The knowledge you have had for years can actually be used to create a multitude of books and teachings for others to learn from and it can be an amazing, beautiful scenario for everyone involved. Now that you've created and generated your chapters, you'll be able to move onto the subject- your themes and book cover and characters.

Organizing chapters can be difficult at first however, it does get easier end it is not that hard to put together themes and ideas that you'd like to write about using an effective outline technique. You can also always change the chapter names as you create them if they're not to your liking.

CHAPTER 3

THE CREATIVE PROCESS

The creative process is an integral process as far as being a writer concerned, and it allows you to be the creative and ideal person that you were truly meant to be. In order to harvest the creative process within yourself and improve enhance and to get it going you will need to focus on many aspects in your life and mind and visualize these many concepts to occur as well.

The creative process is an integral and amazing process by which a writer and creative person gets together and learns how to utilize and harness their gifts. It allows them to do this the best they can in order to be able to influence and help others with the things that are needing to accomplish. In order to be an effective and great writer, you will need to utilize the creative and writing process and be able to focus on your abilities as a writer and grow into someone who is a natural at this.

You'll also want to ask when you write your book who your audience is going to be, for then you can determine who you want to write your book to. Is your audience the normal age group of adults or are you writing a book aimed for teenagers to read? What is the subject matter of the books you're writing about? You'll need to figuratively come up with ideas and brainstorm on how to write your book based on your audience, for they will be the ones who will be buying and reading your books. It's good to know your target audience, for then you can come up with clearer and more concise themes based on the specific people who you feel will be reading your work.

There are five basic steps involved in the creative process and they can be linked to writing

Step 1: Preparation

This is the brainstorming stage of the creative process. You'll have to allow your mind to wander and try to find any kind of inspiration. You can get your inspiration from within your own creative mind or from looking at work from other artists or writers who you look up to. You then can gather the material you'll need to begin putting it all together.

Step 2: Incubation

Stage two of the creative process is involved with walking away from all of the brainstorming a person has just done. While you take a break from the ideas and do other things, your subconscious mind will begin to shape and mold all of the newly found information into your new idea and allow things to come into fruition.

Step 3: Illumination

This is the stage that is most exciting for people. This is the 'eureka' moment where your idea or objective moves from your subconscious mind to the forefront of your mind. Ideas may come to you while doing other things in your daily life such as laundry, driving, studying etc. Ideas will come pouring out to you in different phases and you'll have to learn to write them down as they come to you.

Stage 4: Evaluation

Once the idea of your work or piece of art has been generated or thought of, this stage involves thinking about the newly formed idea and comparing it to other solutions. You can do this by receiving feedback from others or people close to you, conducting research to test the idea, or comparing it to other solutions. If you aren't confident about your new creative thoughts or the subject matter you've come up, you will want to return to stages one and two. You can do this until you come up with a great idea that you love and agree with.

Stage 5: Verification

The final stage of the creative process is where you bring your idea to life or fruition. During this phase, you will begin to write your idea, create a story, and begin the writing process. This is the phase of the creative process where you'll finally want to start being creative and putting all your ideas into words, statements, or any form of art and is the most beautiful and cherished part of being a creative person.

There are many other methods used in the creative process that can be pertained to writing. Although the writing process consists of coming up with drafts and revising, there are other methods a person can use to effectively come up with solid ideas and techniques that will help aid them to be more creative, and that will allow them to become better writers, effectively brainstorm and come up with brand new ideas and thoughts and use their current ideas to put together a good piece of work.

Visualization techniques

Visualization techniques allow a person to really look at the whole picture and the bigger picture. You will need to visualize the aspects you're wanting to write about and the story you want to create. If you have an idea or thought, you'll want to really try to see what it looks like from an outsider's perspective and determine how you want the outcome to be.

Believing in yourself

It's imperative to believe in yourself, your beliefs, ideas, values and your talents and craft. Not everyone has it in them to believe in their own abilities and many people tend to doubt themselves in many given situations and aren't sure how they perceive themselves overall. Do you have hidden talents or gifts that you know about? Do you possess talents or gifts that you're aware of that you have not yet utilized?

You'll want to try to tap into these talents and utilize these abilities of yours in order to succeed as a writer and to gain confidence in general in what you have to speak and write to others. Increasing your confidence levels will allow you to believe in yourself in many forms and let you be a more successful and effective writer and person.

Social and written confidence

You'll need to have social confidence as a writer and written confidence too. Now what is written confidence- it is just the confidence you have as a writer which is needed to be able to generate many types of manuscripts and written art works which you will need to do in order to become a gifted talented person. You'll want people to look up to you and to use your written talent as a means to influence or help people in various ways.

Social confidence is needed to be able to market your material effectively to others, and you'll need to learn marketing techniques in order to be able to do this. You will need to be confident and outgoing when around other people and know exactly what to say and how to showcase your books and talents to them.

Practicing being an incredibly socially confidence can help you become a better writer in general. It can help you become confident in all areas in life, for any form of confidence can allow you to grow in confidence in different forms and in anything that you commit to and partake in.

Writing and practicing often

You'll want to write and write very often and practice a lot and be able to put your ideas together in written format and be a creative, brilliant person and go on from there. The more you write, the better your writing becomes, and this will help you grow. Also, learn from other writers by reading their works and observing their writing skills and abilities and seeing how they put material and information together. This will allow you to hone into your own skills and abilities, develop them further, and become a master and skilled writer at your craft.

Loving yourself and pushing yourself

Love yourself first and foremost and appreciate who you are and what you bring to the table. You'll want to love yourself and focus on who you are and the good and talent you can bring to yourself, your family, friends and to the world. You'll be showcasing your talent to the world so it would need to be perfect and brilliant, and you'll want to appreciate and love yourself for all the great things you do possess and how you seek to help others as well.

You'll want to push yourself into being a better person, a better writer and improving your writing abilities. You can easily push yourself into doing better in writing and doing something great for yourself. This will allow you to ease into the writing process more effectively and become a more creative person.

The Writing Process

The writing process consists of five stages: prewriting, drafting, revising, editing and publishing. These steps allow for a person to come up with ideas and techniques to use while brainstorming an idea and then revising and editing their material and further publishing their work after the necessary steps have been done to ensure a perfect and flawless manuscript and piece of work.

Prewriting

This is the initial phase where the writer comes up with ideas and generates the basis of the piece they are writing about. This includes brainstorming, outlining ideas and organizing thoughts and putting them together. Prewriting is the foundation for the writing process which involves writers putting their thoughts together, organizing ideas, helps make clear their ideas and main purpose.

Drafting

This is the process of the writer putting together the first draft or several different drafts of a piece of work. The idea is to create a rough version of the first draft based on what was initially thought about during the pre-writing phase. Drafts are very important pieces in writing for a writer will usually need to not only write a first draft but put together several ones after revising and editing in order to put together a decent piece of work and one that is polished and written well without any real errors and it's of grave importance to have written several drafts of a book.

Revising

After completing the draft, the writer steps back to revise and review the content thoroughly. This involves making structural changes to the writing, refining the organization, clarifying ideas, and improving the flow of the work. Revising is crucial for enhancing the coherence and effectiveness of the writing.

In order to effectively revise a draft, read it with purpose, focus on the overall structure, clarity and coherence of the draft. You'll want to look for areas that need more detail, get rid of unnecessary content, and make sure that your ideas flow in a rational manner. You also want to make sure that everything makes sense, and the grammatical structuring and content is done properly.

Editing

Editing is a detailed revision process done on a book that includes correcting grammar, punctuation, spelling, and other aspects of the writing. It corrects sentence issues and makes sure that the language is precise, coherent, clear and free of any errors. It enhances the professionalism and overall quality of the work of art.

Editing improves the overall content, quality and structure of the book, while proofreading is the final step that involves checking for errors like spelling, grammar and punctuation.

Some effective editing techniques include taking a break, reading aloud which can help identify awkward phrasing and errors, focusing on structure of the content, checking for clarity, which involves simplifying complex sentences and eliminating jargon whenever possible. Using editing tools such as Grammarly or Hemingway to catch errors and improve readability can also assist with the editing process.

Publishing

Publishing is the final step in the writing and creative process and involves preparing the written work for its audience. This includes formatting, proofreading, and making any final adjustments. Publishing includes the physical and digital production of the work and marketing and promoting it to ensure it reaches people in the correct format. Publishing is about presenting the polished and refined piece to the world, whether it's through traditional print, online platforms, or other means.

You'll want to make sure your work is 100% edited to perfection, has been proofread thoroughly and is completely refined and has been revised in the best way possible, before you format it and make it look pretty and are able to showcase it to the world. Formatting is simply giving the piece of work style and organizing the text and elements to make sure of consistency and readability, by selecting certain fonts, margins, headings and an overall layout.

CHAPTER 4

THEMES AND SENTENCE STRUCTURE

Creating Themes

If you're writing a non-fiction book, you'll want to easily come up with themes, a book outline and structure, and ideas to outline and plot what you plan on writing the book to be about. A non-fiction book might be a little easier to write than a fictional book, because you don't have to create characters or storylines, just gather information you know of and put it together using the information that you do have which is knowledge, wisdom and practical advice and information on the subject.

You'll want to come up with a theme for the book and a subject matter. There are many varying themes you can come up with when it comes to the topics you'd like to write a book about. Can you think of things you have a lot of knowledge of or things you know about? What exactly interests you? If you can come up with an idea or subject matter for the book, then you're well on your way to doing an excellent job with coming up with a decent idea on what to write about.

Is there something you have a specific knowledge of or a lot of knowledge about? Do you know a lot about specific subjects? You'll definitely want to start from there. Do you own a pet and know how to take care of it or feed it and what to do if you need help with the situation? If you do- you can utilize that information to in fact help and assist others with that specific situation using the knowledge and information you've had from your own given experiences. There are so many different topics and ideas you can actually write about! From your dating experiences, to work related situations, there are all kinds of books and subjects that a person has the capability of writing about yet has little information when it comes to knowing this.

If you're wanting to write a self-help book, you can come up with the topic and idea on what to write about and begin to come up with an outline and a storyline you'd like to use for the book. Once you've done that, you can come up with chapter names and themes for the chapters. Once you have named your chapters, you're well on your way to being able to write about the subject matter at hand.

For instance, if you were wanting to write a book on how to take care of a cat, you may want to start off with chapters and titles that begin with the beginnings of caring for a cat, and then work your way down to the end of where you'd like to book to be at. It's really not that difficult to put chapters together- all it takes is a little bit of thinking and slight brainstorming and you should easily be able to come up with the ideas necessary to assist you with putting together an effective and wonderful book idea and outline to start off your project.

Are you writing a fiction or non-fiction book?
Fictional Books

Characters and concepts are a centralized part in a fictional work of art, and you will want to learn how to create and develop these characters if you want to write this specific kind of book. Characters are an integral part of the story and something that need to be created and developed very effectively in order to be able to write a good story. Characters are generally found in fictional works and if you're going to write this kind of novel, you will need to come up with characters in your story, names of characters and different themes associated with these people. Have you thought about the first book you're wanting to write and the kinds of characters you're interested in writing about? Are you a creative person or have you ever put together ideas for a book or thought about creating the people that you're going to use for a storyline. Creating characters takes time and practice and it's something that can't be done right away. You are someone learning to be a gifted talented writer and using your talents in the best way that you can.

Every story has a theme, and you'll need to create a theme associated with your book and storyline. What theme did you want your book or story to be associated with? Have you thought about exactly what you'd like to focus on when it comes to the storyline of the book? Don't worry! Every person has to start somewhere, and this is exactly where you'll have to focus on being very creative and focus on your talents and gifts. There are ways of enhancing your creative energy and that is by tapping into your hidden gifts, talents, and the energies that are a part of your inner self. Many writers write through their mind, their brain and use their mental capacity in a very effective manner, but there are also energetic forces at play a lot of the times when it comes to being able to write and be an effective writer and someone who is skilled at their craft. Using your energetic abilities to tap into unseen energetic forces and your own energies can generally enhance your writing capabilities and allow you to become a better and more creative person in general.

Characters in a book or play are in general need of development and you'll want to spend time developing these characters and ideas. You are the master of your creative arts and the works you are creating and will always be the one who can further yourself and your creative abilities by utilizing other tactics and means to be able to further develop your arts and skills.

There are methods for developing characters and some of these methods include:

Developing a background for a character

Knowing your characters strengths and weaknesses

Creating nervous ticks or habits

Characters can't always be perfect

All characters need real motives

Giving characters unique features

Give characters a diverse voice

Create a diverse cast

Try to avoid stereotypes in characters

Ask character development questions

Non-fictional books

Non-fiction books generally have the following characteristics

If you're writing a non-fiction book, you'll want to come up with a particular theme of the book you desire to write.

What exactly do you seek to write about or put together? Do you want to write to help others and be in the self-help genre, or do you want to write non-fictional books about other subjects? Most self-help books do not have characters in them, but they have a centralized theme or subject. Once you've determined the subject you seek to write about, you will want to come up with chapters and ideas first off in order to start off with. The reasoning for this is, once you come up with chapters and ideas, it will be far easier to come up with points and ideas in the book you're putting together. The chapters will be the centralized points of what exactly your book is about, and you can further begin putting together an outline for your book.

Non-fictional books generally have the following characteristics:

Factual content

They present real information, facts and data rather than fictional stories or narratives

Purposeful structure

They often following a clear structure such as chapters or sections or organize information logically and in a concise, readable interesting method

Research-based

Many non-fiction works are in fact research based and based on interviews or firsthand accounts that provide evidence to support claims

Informative tone

They often have an informative tone, and the writing style is often aiming to educate or inform the reader of information and knowledge based themes

Variety of genres

Non-fiction does encompass genres such as memoirs, biographies, self-help essays and instructional information

Sentence Structure and Grammar

Sentence structure is imperative when it comes to putting your book together. How grammatically talented are you? Do you have poor or good English or grammar? If you can easily put together a paragraph of information, then you're golden when it comes to sentence structure when it comes to writing a book and coming up with ideas. When writing a book, you will want to use perfect sentence structure and grammar and will want to proofread your material or use Grammarly or other word/punctuation programs or editors to be able to fully proofread your material or double check for any errors or issues.

Do you know how to put sentences together effectively and have you written for a long time or are you brand new to writing and unsure of how to effectively put together a sentence? What is your grammar like- do you know how to properly use punctuation or other aspects of grammatical abilities. Writing often will allow you to become more knowledgeable about writing, punctuation and grammatical structure and once you've mastered this art, you'll be able to not only effectively write but become a master at revision and it will become much easier for you in the long run.

You're an amazing, talented gifted person and writer and will want to remind yourself of this any chance you can get. You can easily write a book if you so choose to desire and it's not that difficult of a feat for you. If you choose to do so, you can become even better if you continue practicing these writing skills and abilities and focusing on honing your craft any chance you can get.

Grammar and sentence structure should be done in a proper format and utilized effectively through means of proofreading effectively and revising often. Once you're able to proofread and revise, you'll be able to make sure your grammar is exceptionally proper and correct. One way of achieving this is by going over your document regularly and even paying a decent editor to correctly edit your document and proofread it to perfection. This is the only way you will be able to master the concept of perfect sentence structure and grammar and know how to revise your own documents and edit them to perfection yourself. If you don't do this on your own, then your manuscript will more than likely be faulty and will not have the proper grammatical formats needed to be a proper manuscript free of errors.

CHAPTER 5

HOW TO DEVELOP YOUR WRITING ABILITIES

Developing your writing abilities takes hard work, dedication and talent. It's not something that can happen overnight, and it takes years of months of effort and practice. Your writing abilities can be a natural trait or habit for you or actually something that has developed over years of thorough and intricate practice and after years of being able to put together solid works through your skills. Your writing abilities are your hard work, and your gifts utilized together in order to create a perfect and harmonious piece of work or art that you can showcase to the world and to others.

There are many methods for how to develop your abilities. Writing is a great skill and with it comes a great craft and it does take practice and can possibly even help you with other areas in your life that you're lacking confidence in or are unsure of. Are there areas in your life that you need assistance with developing or getting better at? You can generally help yourself become better at writing through other arenas in your life and gain and develop confidence by being a more confident person in general and letting your other abilities and talents allow you to become better at your writing craft.

Are you talented or good in specific areas in your life? Are you good at a certain sport, or maybe a specific arena in your life? Maybe you're very gifted at singing, music or some other area in your world? You can utilize that area to actually write about and use it to develop your craft and your abilities as a writer. By focusing on your positive strengths, you allow yourself to develop in every aspect and portion in your life and reality. You'll be well on your way to helping develop your writing abilities and become a better writer in general.

Writing development is a craft and artform and is comprised of many different facets

How to develop your writing abilities:

Master the art of sentence structure and proper grammar

It's imperative to be able to master the fine art of sentence structure and proper grammar and punctuation. To do this, you will want to write often, and practice writing different forms and types of writing. You will want to proofread very often and be thorough with your proofreading and revising and know exactly what is proper sentence structure and grammar. Once you've thoroughly studied the concept of structure of sentences and good grammar and punctuation, you'll be on your way to becoming a more natural writer and something that will come to you more easily as opposed to someone who might be struggling in their writing.

Focus on your positive strengths

We all have positive strengths and good notions and ideas in our life. We often tend to take for granted the things we are good at and don't let them become incorporated into our everyday life and put them in the back burner. This is something that shouldn't be done at all. We need to focus on the things that we're generally good at or have been successful in. This will help build our inner confidence and let us become stronger people in general and even allow us to become better writers and better at what we're currently doing.

Practice regularly

Write consistently through journals, blogging, or workshops and by doing creative writing exercises. Write essays and exchange writing critiques with other fellow writers. Gain ideas from other on how they write and the techniques they use. Practice as often as you can and don't hold back- write as much as possible for it will allow you to develop your abilities and skills very effectively and become an even better writer than you could possibly imagine.

Read often

Expose yourself to different authors, styles and genres to understand people's writing techniques. Read what you want to write. Read the news or grab a book to read for most of the day. Start with topics you're interested in and begin to know the authors and genres that you enjoy. Reading the topics and writings of other talented authors gives you great insight and perspective into how they write and will allow you to become open to their styles of writing and the manner by which they effectively put their work together. It will give you great insight into the varying perspectives of different aspects on writing and allow you to become a better writer in general and let your workflow with success.

Ask for feedback

Share your work with others and fellow peers to receive constructive criticism and gain new perspectives and ideas on your writing and how you can improve or what errors might be present there. Getting feedback from others can greatly help a person improve and correct any errors that might be present in their writing abilities and allows them to receive the best constructive criticism that they need in order to help them become more effective and better writers in general.

Study writing techniques

Study various writing techniques, styles and how other writers tend to put their work together. Learn about grammar, sentence structure and style through workshops, writing courses and books. Studying different techniques will allow you to experiment with your current writing skills and abilities and help determine if you need to adopt a better writing style in order to allow your writing to become greater and improve and possess better types and styles.

Edit and revise

Embrace the editing process to refine and improve your work and make it appear better.

Editing is an extremely important part of the writing process, and the more you edit your work, the better it becomes and the more it stands out to others. You'll want your work of art to be perfection and the more you work at it the better it will be. Editing is one of the most important aspects of being a successful and great writer and you'll want to edit your work often to make sure that there are no discrepancies or errors in it and that it is something you have created to perfection. The editing and revision process can easily be learned in a few simple steps and will also need to be done on a regular basis.

Embrace who you are as a writer

Embrace your writing skills and your style. You will want to embrace who you are as a writer and appreciate all the little and fine things about yourself. Once you embrace yourself as a writer, you'll far more easily be able to put together the best books, works of writing and improve your sentence structure and thought patterns by which you do write with. Embracing who you are as a wonderful writer will further allow you to develop your skills and gifts and bring up your confidence levels drastically. You are a talented, gifted writer and will want to remind yourself of this at all times and teach yourself these concepts on a regular basis.

Repeat Positive Affirmations and Mantras

It's important to repeat positive affirmations and statements toward yourself on a daily basis. These will help enhance your creative abilities and build your confidence when it comes to becoming a good or decent writer. Positive affirmations are a very important and amazing tool to help someone embrace growth and increase their confidence levels when it comes to writing or in any area in your life.

I am a great writer who can overcome any challenge

I can easily put a book together

I have natural writing talents and abilities

I that putting a book together is an easy task for me

Once I begin to write more, it will become much easier for me

I am a success at whatever I do

Writing success comes easily to me, I can write with ease

CHAPTER 6

FEARS AND ANXIETIES REGARDING WRITING

Many people may have fears and anxieties when it comes to writing. They aren't sure how to go about it or might be confused in general as to how to create a book, write about it or put it together. Having fears about writing is very normal but it's important to be able to thwart those fears and not let them ruin your abilities or your abilities to write in general. What do people generally have fears about. The most important aspect of being a writer is the idea that you're actually a great, interesting and successful writer who actually has the ability to write a book and put one together effectively, and that you've done so successfully and done very well at it. For most writers, the beauty of being able to write and put their work together and have people read it is the true and ultimate epitome of being a gifted and good writer, not necessarily other aspects regarding it such as winning awards or being a best-seller.

You should never have fears when it comes to writing for fear itself is a huge problem for so many people. Fears can generate negative outcomes for writers such as writing block, unintelligible writing and stories or concepts that just aren't as good as if a person didn't have the notion of fear somewhere within them. Writing a book might seem like a daunting task but it really should be a very exciting journey a person is undergoing similar to running a marathon, and it does take practice and skill that a person is able to develop over a number of years through practice or other means such as writing lessons, or more writing. Having unfounded fears when it comes to being a writer can hamper your ability to create decent and good books and can ruin your skills in the long run and create major anxieties inside yourself, psyche, and mind

You'll need to have a clear mind when writing and possess confidence within yourself. Being a writer can be a very difficult thing for a person and with it comes many fears which are self-created or simply just there for most people who are writers.

Writers are often plagued with all types of unfounded fears and issues associated with their writing abilities. They believe in all sorts of delusional ideas with regards to their writing skills that are untrue, and it presents and can create real problems and issues in their hobbies and writing careers.

Fear of failure

Many writers have a fear of failure in many aspects of their writing skills. They are often afraid they just won't succeed or do well, or that they've made too many mistakes in their manuscript, they fear they may never see their books in a store, fear they won't ever be traditionally published. They also feel as if they just won't do well as a writer, won't ever win awards or won't be recognized for their writing abilities or that no one will ever like or buy their books. This is very normal for a writer to have these kinds of fears in their writing career or in their life, and it's normal to ponder upon these ideations though these aspects of writing aren't as important.

Fear of Shame

Many writers have a fear of shame, which typically has to do with standards that other people set and how you feel others perceive you. Many writers are worried and feel scared they might be outcasted, judged, mocked or put down for the things they've written about, though this is definitely not the perspective you'll ever want to take. If that thought never graced your mind, you'll want to not worry too much about it, for being a writer is allowing you to express your opinions and shine them onto the world in the most creative and effective amazing way possible, which is the real reason people are writers and authors and showcase themselves to the world through written word.

Many writers want to be perfect at their art and display perfection and be the greatest they can be. They seek to be the best in their genre and when they aren't, they feel as if they are lesser than what their ideals are. Writers fear they won't live up to their own ideals or to the ideals others have of them.

Fear of self-delusion

Some writers fear self-delusion and fear they aren't even writers or real writers. It's a very unfortunate scenario that tends to happen to some creative people out there. They feel they've been fooling themselves all along and aren't what or who they thought they are. Some writers also feel they don't have the writing skills to be considered good or great writers and feel as if their work isn't good enough or is mediocre. This is a common occurrence among writers.

Fear of obscurity

Many writers are afraid of just being an unknown writer and someone whose books aren't even read or known. This does happen to many writers, and they are literally unknown and do not have many customers or readers when it comes to their works or books. This is an unfortunate scenario for writers as the most important aspect of being a writer encompasses that of the beauty and joy of writing and being able to be an effective and decent writer out there, not the worries of being obscure or an unknown writer. It does take time for a person to be known and even if it doesn't happen it's definitely not the worst-case scenario for any writer. Writing a book is a huge accomplishment and this is what a writer should focus on, not the accomplishments and accolades that should come with being a writer.

Imposter syndrome: The fear of being exposed as a fraud

Perfectionism: Fretting over every detail

Judgment fear: Being nervous about upsetting others

Fear of rejection: Fear of people rejecting their words

Fear of writing a dull book: Fear of writing something that isn't interesting

Fear of being too literary: Fear of writing something that is too literary

Fear of rehashing characters: Fear of writing the same characters descriptions and dialogue many times.

Fear of writing something boring: Fear of writing something that isn't interesting

Fear of contradicting facts or character traits: Fear of writing something that contradicts facts or character traits

Writers can often overcome fears by setting real goals, getting feedback from trusted people in their life, practicing self-care and compassion, establishing a good routine, revising their work often and focusing on the good aspects of writing rather than trying to be perfect and focusing on the negative or fears of it.

Routine allows writers to gain structure and discipline and helps them establish a consistent writing habit that can enhance creativity and allows them to be productive in their goals and abilities. It also reduces anxiety greatly, by creating a familiar environment where good ideas can come through more freely.

Many writers have harsh criticisms about themselves or their writing abilities. they feel as if they just aren't good enough, aren't living up to their own standards or those of others. It's imperative to stray from criticizing yourself or your abilities for that creates self-doubt and will reflect in your writing and make you unsure of yourself and the things you're putting out. You'll want to be sure of yourself and focus on the positives that you do possess, rather than feel as if you're just not good enough or not doing as decently as you want to be doing.

Never allow your fears to take over you or affect your writing style or hamper your ability to write. It can be difficult sometimes, but you will need to build your confidence levels and continue to write- this will allow and assist you to become a better writer in general and allow you to improve your writing skills and abilities. You possess a wonderful gift and have the ability to enhance it and can use it to send a message to the world, to help others, to improve people's lives and so much more. Never sell yourself short or believe that you're not good enough, because you are far better than you believe yourself to be.

CHAPTER 7

BELIEVING IN YOUR WRITING ABILITIES

Writing is a beautiful art form, and it can also be a natural method that people use to put their works and words together in order to create an influential and enigmatic piece for people to read and become interested in. It is a succinct form of creativity and can be utilized in many forms.

You too can be a great writer if you truly put hard work and dedication into this craft and use your skills wisely and learn how to put together words and sentences effectively in cohesively in order to create a wonderful masterpiece that you can share with the world. One key aspect of being a great writer is focusing on the confidence you harness within your own self. It can be the difference between being a great writer and someone who is mediocre, and you'll want to bring your confidence up on a constant level in order to put out the kinds of writings you'd love the world to embrace.

Confidence is key when it comes to writing and when it comes to being an effective talented gifted and influential writer. You can't just write a book without having some form of confidence within you. It will help you tremendously to learn how to develop your confidence in various forms if you want to further develop abilities.

Not everyone believes in their abilities or in their ability to be a good writer. Writers in general have many doubts about themselves and some aren't sure they're even good writers or are unsure about how audiences will perceive them or receive their work.

Writers can sometimes be some of the most hesitant and self-judgmental people in any given field yet and they are some of the most gifted talented people to exist. It's imperative that you don't fall in the negative category of being one of those people who thinks in a negative format rather than in a very positive one. It's easy to fall into the trap of being a negative person, rather than one who is incredibly positive, but in order to be a successful writer, you'll have to focus on being a very positive person with a beneficial state of mind. Writers are gifted wonderful special people who are generally gifted with the ability to put together magical words and special creative energies in order to influence and help others and the masses.

In order to truly believe in your writing abilities and in yourself you'll have to greatly elevate your confidence levels and your self-esteem. There are a multitude of ways to increase and elevate your self-esteem. You'll want to bring yourself up all of the time and believe in you and your own creative abilities. This takes time to do but once you do well and are successful at doing what you do, then you'll develop more and more abilities your confidence will skyrocket and become greatly elevated.

It's very important to believe in your own special abilities and in the talents and gifts that you partake in, for if you do not believe in yourself and your own abilities, then it will be extremely difficult for you to master the creative process in the art of writing and for you to get started as a writer and continue this process.

Believing in your abilities and yourself takes confidence and self-esteem it takes a greater understanding of yourself and your own talents and the things that you do possess within yourself. You are an integral part of this society and can do a lot of greatness and helping of others and this is something that you may not know. A writer is a great part of this creative and wonderful process, and you can actually help and heal many people using your creative writing abilities and getting your message out there to others and being of wonderful help and healing towards people in general and spreading the knowledge that you do possess to others so the others can learn, and intern help others as well with the knowledge that they are gaining from what you are writing.

You will need to gain confidence within yourself in order to be able to write and spread your message through written word and be able to focus on yourself and your abilities as a writer so that you can relay your message through written word towards others with confidence, love kindness, and goodness and be able to spread your beautiful wonderful message to the masses and to the world out there.

It's very easy to believe in yourself to gain confidence in yourself. Focus on the positives that you do have and all the wonderful blessings that you have in your world and your life for there are so many things that you should be proud of and things about yourself that you should build upon and cherish.

The creative process is the most important one and it's important to be able to understand all the creative abilities that you do possess within yourself and the abilities that you are able to actually tap into. Most of us possess creative abilities, and talents, that we are unaware of that we were actually able to tap into using our own inner thoughts and energies.

There are various characteristics you'll need to have in order to be a successful and effective writer and to hone into your creative abilities in a greater manner

1. Patience: patience is of utmost value when it comes to being a talented and decent writer in the world of writing. Your skill level matters too, but it is good to possess an abundance of patience, for as a writer, you'll be sitting at a computer for hours on end writing tediously and will want to have the concept of patience within them and will want to learn to develop this wondrous characteristic and trait.
2. Virtue: you'll want to have virtue within yourself as a writer simply because virtue allows you to have moral standards by which you write and as a writer, you'll need to possess an abundance of these morals and standards for this is the method and manner by which you'll want to abide by the rules and regulations of the planet in order to put together works of written art in order to move and help others in a substantiated amazing format.
3. Tolerance: you'll need tolerance as a writer simply because tolerance allows you to wait and patiently sit and think of ideas, characters,

concepts and the ideas you'll need to effectively create a decent book and work of art.
4. Creativity: creativity is an important element and asset that is needed in order to be a creative book writer and in order to do something positive within your field of work. You'll need to hone in on your inner skills and your mental acuity and fulfill your creativity in many different formats in order to be a gifted and talented skilled writer in this field.

Elevate your confidence levels

Focus on being positive rather than negative

Sometimes as writers it's easy to get down on us. People end up having issues with their writing, there is negativity in their world, or they come up with roadblocks and other problems in general. People can grow to become negative, though they should stay positive and it's of major importance that a person is extremely positive towards times of negativity and during times of tribulations in their life.

Believe in yourself and focus on your strengths

You will need to have a great amount of confidence and have a strong belief in yourself and your abilities, strengths and talents as a writer. It's easy to get down on ourselves, feel as if we're not good enough or simply just can't do as good of a job as we want on something. Many times, people just don't have the belief in themselves that they can do well or succeed. You will want to have a very strong belief in yourself and your talents and abilities as a writer for your belief in your talents can boost your self-esteem and elevate your confidence in a huge and grand way.

Focus on all the positive aspects of yourself, your strengths and the wonderful qualities you do possess, and you'll find yourself doing well and improving in your writing ability and doing a great job when it comes to writing and your creativity will skyrocket as well. What aspects of writing are you good at? What areas in your life are you successful at? If you're good at creating characters, then pat yourself on the back for being able to have this ability and strength and move on from there. Positivity does create more positivity, and it snowballs, so once you're confident and glad that you're good at one thing, you can start to gain confidence in areas you may not feel you're good in and move on from there.

Set reasonable expectations

As a writer, you will always want to set reasonable expectations of yourself. You won't want to write thinking that you can write the best or be the best writer, but you'll want to write with the notion that you're continuously wanting to improve and be the best writer that you can be.

Set expectations for yourself. You don't want to write a book too fast or even sell yourself short. You will want to make sure that your writing is at a fair and decent pace and that you've done all that you can to become the best writer you can be. You also don't want to believe or feel that you can write a book or novel in a very short period of time, so you need to set a time frame or period by which you can actually have your work of art done by. You are a gifted, talented capable person who is able to do many different things in your life and writing isn't the only thing you're capable of accomplishing.

In order to be a success at writing, you'll want to elevate your abilities and focus on different methods for doing so, and this is very reasonable for anyone to accomplish or achieve.

Have a social network of people to support you

You should feel supported in everything that you do and that's why it's of good importance to have social groups and people in your life who can support you and cheer you on and encourage you. You are a very important person, and your writing journey is of utmost importance. It is important for you to harness your abilities and be able to share them with others through written word. You will have most likely been practicing a long time with your talents and abilities and doing an exceptional good job and working at this for a long time. Having a wonderful social support system will enable you to succeed in the long run and gain constant praise and support which will increase your confidence levels in a major way.

Repeat positive affirmations constantly and daily

Positive affirmations are a great tool to assist someone in building their confidence levels and assisting someone with becoming better at their craft and in elevating their skills. It's a good idea to repeat mantras and write out positive affirmations and repeat them to yourself on a daily basis, so you can build your confidence and become a better, happier and more whole person and improve as a writer by utilizing your inner belief in yourself.

I am a great writer who can overcome any challenge

I can easily put a book together

I have natural writing talents and abilities

I that putting a book together is an easy task for me

Once I begin to write more, it will become much easier for me

Writing comes easily and naturally to me

I am the best writer out there, and can easily put a manuscript together

I believe in my abilities as a writer, and my vocabulary is unlimited

Believing in your writing abilities

I have the ability to study and learn different types of writing techniques

Chapter 8

Enhancing Your Writing Abilities

Enhancing your writing abilities, takes great and appealing skill, and it takes years of practice to be able to do. When you first start off, you are just a beginner, and your writing abilities may not be as great as you want them to be. You will have to learn to practice putting sentences together, ideas, concepts, and themes. For many beginners, this is a different a very difficult task to do because they don't feel as if they're capable or or able to put together coherent and cohesive sentences and use proper grammatical structure. However, many people's fears about writing can be eliminated and eradicated easily once they begin the writing process. Now what is the writing process you may ask? The writing process is actually the method by which you begin writing as a beginner and you gradually start to get better and better the more you write and the more works you put together.

It may seem scary and difficult at first. I know that many years ago I was incredibly terrified and felt as if writing a book was a very difficult task to do. Organizing the chapters seemed very difficult as well. However, I learned that after writing my first book and my second book everything became much easier.

In fact, creating chapters and my first book was not difficult as at all. The problem with this scenario is that there is a perception that all of this is incredibly difficult, but the reality is that putting all of this together- the chapter, the book is actually a very simple task to do, though it seems difficult through the lens of a person who has never done it.

Once you actually put your first book together, you gradually learn that this is not a very difficult process and the more you do it the easier it becomes. It seems perception a very difficult process for a person who has never done it before. Enhancing a person's writing abilities takes talent and writing skill, and is something that someone can do after writing many various works of art and perfecting these works of art. The more writing you do the better you get at it and the greater you will be, just like any other art or hobby that a person can partake in.

As a beginner writer of a material such as a book or novel, you will need to understand and comprehend, and know the most difficult part of writing a book is actually getting started and facing your fears of feeling as if this task is extremely difficult and something that you're unable to accomplish, when in reality, it is really not that difficult and something that you can do once you get started on it and get past your fears of getting started. For most people, it is the fear of writing and getting started and being unable to accomplish this that stops them from being writers in the first place or attempting to write a book.

Once you finally hurdle this obstacle, you will be well on your way to being a successful and accomplished writer and author, and putting together a book will be very simple for you. You will learn to become a master at doing this because once you're able to overcome these major obstacles of writing, he will be able to easily put together a manuscript and a novel, writing a book will be incredibly exciting and easy for you to achieve and partake in.

What kind of writer are you? There are many types of writers out there and you will want to try to figure out what type of writer you are. Are you a fiction writer who creates imaginative stories or novels, or are you a non-fiction writer who focuses on factual content such as journalists or biographies? Are you a poet or a technical writer? You'll need to figure out what kind of writer you seek to be and what kind of work you'd like to do in the field of writing.

Enhancing and being able to improve your writing abilities and skills as an exciting and challenging scenario for anyone to be a part of and to partake in. You may have a natural knack for writing or you may not have many abilities at all, but the beauty of writing is that once you actually begin doing it, you gain greater abilities for yourself and for your work and pretty soon you will find yourself to be an expert and master in the world and art of writing and will be practicing and honing your skill just like any other hobby or career or arena that a person may be a part of.

Enhancing your writing abilities is definitely not something that can be done right away. You can become a better writer simply by writing or by utilizing your creative abilities the best that you can. Being a great writer takes the art of practice, practice, and practice. You can never write too much, for the more you write, the better you become.

There are many ways of enhancing your beautiful creative skills. Creativity comes from the core of your heart and from the center of your soul and it is a extreme importance and imperative that you enhance it. Any chance you can get in by different means.

Creativity is the essence of our souls, and you are a beautiful special spirit, beautiful special person by being able to be a gifted and good writer.

Creativity is the essence of our soul, and we need to enhance our confidence levels and our personal power and inner core in order to be able to improve our writing abilities.

You are a gifted, talented writer, and someone who also aspires to be this kind of success as a writer. Not everyone is a talented writer to start off with, though many people might be naturally gifted with the ability of writing. Improving our writing abilities, actually comes from writing frequently and very frequently and being able to learn from our past mistakes and being effective learners of new writing techniques and strategies.

We need to learn how to become better writers through our writing journey. We can become successes once we focus on the more important aspects of our life which includes focusing on the small successes and gaining confidence and loving ourselves unconditionally.

Building upon our confidence and positivity

Building upon your confidence and positivity is one of the few ways you can enhance your writing abilities and become better at what you do. Our confidence within ourselves is of extreme importance when it comes to the writing process, and we will need to possess good amounts of it in order to become an effective and decent writer and allow our successes and abilities to affect other areas of our lives which it usually does and let us grow in our confidence and allow us to do anything we possibly can. The sky is truly the limit for you when you learn to build upon your confidence and positivity.

Proofread and Effective Editing

Do an effective job of proofreading and being able to go over the manuscript and the text and be able to be a master at proofing your writing and the writing of others. Many people do not publish their works until they have proofread their work at least a minimum of three to four times or even more. The more you proofread your work, the better chances you can catch any errors and even improve upon your sentences, grammatical structuring, and the manner in which you write, or any errors that are present in your manuscript.

Get feedback about your books

It's imperative to get feedback about your books your manuscript and everything that you have written. There are ways of getting beta readers to read your books before they are published. you want to get and write down and understand the opinions that others have of your writing and the whole hearted earnest feedback that she received from others and utilize it to the best of your knowledge and understanding.

It's not difficult to find unbiased readers who can give you a plethora of advice and opinions about your writing and give you the advice you need in order to be able to enhance your writing skills, improve your writing, and correct any errors that may be present.

Focus on structure in writing

Structure is a very important variable when it comes to writing, and you will want to improve your sentence and overall structure in order to be able to create a much better product than you currently have.

Structure in writing is about forming an outline will help solidify the writing. An outline can clarify what you hope to convey in each section, allowing you to visualize the flow of your piece and surface parts that require more research or thought. Outlines are very important if you're wanting an organized method for creating your book, for without it, you generally have a haphazard manuscript, and it can leave you confused and unsure of what to write.

The structure might look different depending on what you're writing. An essay typically has an introduction, body, paragraph, and a conclusion.

Write as often as possible

Writing more and more often helps you improve your writing abilities and skills. Writing is a form of art and therapy, and you will need a lot of practice in order to become a better writer and a more gifted person in this field. You will want to write more often and write different kinds of pieces for the more you write the better skills and abilities you have as a writer and the better writer you will end up being.

You may not understand the writing process to start off with, but the more you write and the more pieces of art and work you put out there, the greater your writing abilities will become and the greater enhanced they will end up becoming in general. Write as much as you can and practice the manner in which other writers write as well and the methods and processes, they use. This will give you varying and differing perspectives on your own writing and allow you to become better at your craft.

CHAPTER 9

STAYING TRUE TO YOURSELF

Being an effective writer means staying true to yourself and your beliefs. Your values are ideal, and everything that you stand for once you do this then you're going to be able to effectively relay all the wonderful knowledge and gifts and talents that you actually possess and written words so that it can spread to those around you and others can learn and from reading your written knowledge.

Do you know your beliefs and ideals, and the things that you actually believe in and all the values that you hold near and dear to yourself or are these concepts, oblivious to you? Have you pondered upon the concepts that you truly believe in? If you haven't, it's important to do some self-examining and introspection upon self in order to understand who you really are and what morals and ideals you live by and the standards that you live by and believe in.

Staying true to your beliefs and ideals, is your thoughts and ideas existing and then being able to enmesh themselves into written words so that you can speak to others through your books and through your writings. You will always want to focus on your own inner beliefs and what you feel is right or true and spread your knowledge and word to others in an amazing and great way.

This helps with better decision making. You can make better decisions as a writer and pursue your goals as a writer if you stay true to yourself and your ideals and values. You'll also have less regret as a writer if you stay aligned with your beliefs and passions and you can have a greater influence in your writing and the aspects you speak about in your books and through your words.

You'll be a better book writer if you choose to stay true to yourself and live through the lens of your beliefs and what you hold near and dear to you. You'll feel stronger and more confident in the decisions you make, and you will also not regret the decisions you make with regards to situations and scenarios you've chosen to do.

You'll eliminate the concept of people pleasing or living by someone else's standards or rules. You just live as your natural self without any compromise. Many writers are people pleasers who feel as if they need to worry about what others think of them or how they write. Some feel as if they are literary enough and others feel as if they just aren't good enough. If you learn how to build your confidence by living up to your own standards, you won't worry about wanting to do it for others.

Better decision-making is about being honest with yourself and allows you to pursue really great goals as a writer. Being true to yourself is pursuing your goals and dreams as a gifted, talented writer and being able to influence others with the message you put out and your beautiful gift of words and beliefs.

What are your goals as a writer?

What are your goals as a writer? How do you plan on pursuing your writing talent and what kind of books or art do you plan to write or relay to others? Do you plan on pursuing other goals in your life or do you plan on being a writer only? It's important to have goals in life and know exactly what you plan on doing as far as what genre of book you plan on writing and presenting to others.

How do you plan on enhancing your writing abilities?

How much experience do you have as a writer? Have you written short stories, novellas or even more? It's of great importance that you enhance your writing abilities if you're able to. You can take workshops to improve your writing abilities and attempt to write different types of books than you're normally used to in order to create diversity in your writing, enhance your abilities and give yourself more experience as a writer.

Do you know about the creative process?

The creative process is a natural process by which you can create art, short stories, books and other works of art through your creative abilities and utilize it to benefit yourself and help yourself get better as an artist. Are you a creative person? have you put together works of art before? You'll want to try to hone in on your creative abilities in order to get this process started. Once you become creative and begin writing, you will begin to tap into your writing abilities, and it will become far easier for you to put together pieces of art that you can call 'books' and use these as paraphernalia in your life.

How can you stay true to your beliefs and ideals

1. Tell yourself that you're satisfied with who you are

You'll need to tell yourself that you're satisfied with who you are and always embrace and love yourself and the achievements you've accomplished and that you're good enough for yourself. By focusing on being satisfied with who you are, you can stay true to your real self, rather than changing who you are and being a different person or of a different kind of nature.

It's a great idea to be extremely happy with who you are and focus on building on the strengths that you possess and trying to do more with those strengths and focusing on them only, not on the things you don't have or have obtained.

Stay satisfied and focused on the minor aspects in your work, your writing and focus on the good things that you have obtained. You should be very proud of the work you have done and how you have stayed true to yourself and your beliefs, and you are a strong and amazing person who can handle all that life has to throw at you with ease and grace.

2. Ignore other people's judgments of you

With writing will come a lot of harsh judgments, stereotypes, and all kinds of repeat scenarios of people having criticisms about your work along with other phenomenon. It's important that you embrace who you are as a writer and learn to ignore the critics out there and those who want to put you down or those who feel a specific way towards your writing. You will need to write and stay true to your beliefs and what you stand for and not allow those who judge you to bring your perception of yourself down or change it in any form.

3. Embrace Growth and Change

Embracing growth and change is an integral part of staying true to you and your beliefs for with experience comes growth and you'll really want to embrace this and learn to change with the coming times and situations.

4. Forgive the past

It's a good idea to focus on forgiving the past and any negative circumstances that have ever happened to you. Your life matters and all the things you've experienced that are negative or painful in nature do hold some form of significance. You'll need to let go and forgive the past for this is imperative in order for you to become a stronger and deeper person and be able to really express your opinions creatively the way you need to.

5. Express Yourself Creatively

Believe in yourself: you must believe in yourself and your personal strengths for it is of the essence that will allow you to become stronger within yourself and allow you to develop the confidence and abilities needed in order to become a successful writer and author. Express yourself creatively as best as you can. Attempt to tap into and hone your creative abilities by tapping into your personal energy and your intuitive self. This will assist with the creative process and allow you to become a better creative person and writer in general.

6. Love yourself unconditionally

You will want to love yourself in a very caring and kind manner and have a deep desire to want to do good for yourself and help yourself out. It's important to love yourself no matter what happens and regardless of what you do or what an outcome is.

7. Focus on your strengths

It's good to focus on the strengths you possess and all the positive aspects you do have in your life. You will need to focus on your talents and abilities and list which ones you do have and learn to appreciate them and then go on from utilizing these things in order to better yourself as a good writer and better your abilities.

8. Practice the art of writing

The art of practicing writing is of extreme importance if you want to become a great or good writer and improve your skills and abilities, and you'll want to better yourself in many various methods. Take workshops, classes, and try to improve your skills as you practice different formats of this. Honing your craft is a good idea for it will allow you to improve and become better at what you are doing and allow you to think of different ideas to write about and different writing styles as well.

Accept that change is a part of life and an opportunity for personal growth. Identify one area in your life where you believe that change has taken place and allow yourself to change in that arena so you can become better at your craft.

Are you a great writer naturally or do you need to practice and study the art and craft of writing to become better? We can all improve our writing no matter what our situation is, though naturally talented writers seem to have it easier when coming to the writing process and being able to put together a solid and decent manuscript. You will always want to practice your art skillfully and begin to improve your amazing skills and grow as a writer and write drafts if you can and be the best you can be at this great genre.

There are many methods that can help a person increase the standards for their writing abilities and help to improve their writing. They will want to utilize these methods on a regular basis especially if they aren't a naturally talented writer. Putting together a book seems difficult at first, but once it is done a few times become far easier to do, though does take time, hard work, dedication and practice. It becomes easier to organize the chapters, think of chapter names, create a decent cover and put together a manuscript and body of a work of art.

You will want to learn the various techniques, tips, shortcuts and strategies for doing this in order to become a gifted writer and talented individual and book writer. It's a good idea to tap into your intuitive and creative abilities while you are developing these abilities as well, and you'll be well on your way to being a very successful and published author and having a great career ahead of you.

Staying true to yourself means believing in your own self and your own morals, and the aspects that you hold near and dear to you. It allows you to grow in the social process and elevates your confidence because you understand the different aspects that you grew up with, and we're born within that were talk to you and know how to utilize them in your every day, world and life and stay true to your personal self and power.

Has writing been a difficult journey for you? Did you never feel you could ever write a book or were you confused as to how to get started? You're definitely not the only one who feels this way, for many people out there feel as if writing is a difficult feat for them and something they don't have the talent, gifts, or abilities to undergo or obtain in some form. However, you too can be a great writer and write a book successfully if you only put your mind to it and practice hard work, repetitiveness and dedication.

In order to be a successful writer, it takes hard work, determination and talent to hone your craft and allow your writing career to move forward and for you to become extremely good at this and even win awards and have a number of published books out there.

With writing comes challenges, though you should be able to handle these challenges and overcome any major issues you have faced or dealt with during your journey as a writer. It takes overcoming these challenges and hurdles such as writers block, other people's judgments and writer's harsh criticisms of themselves in order to be able to be successful and do well in your journey and career. You'll want to exude a lot of internal confidence and be happy with yourself and your work in order to do well and exceed expectations.

www.ingramcontent.com/pod-product-compliance
Lightning Source LLC
LaVergne TN
LVHW012033060526
838201LV00061B/4588